A KID'S GUIDE TO BUILDING AND
EXPLORING IN THE GREAT OUTDOORS

Sticks
AND
Stones

MELISSA LENNIG

QUARRY

Brimming with creative inspiration, how-to projects, and useful information to enrich your everyday life, Quarto Knows is a favorite destination for those pursuing their interests and passions. Visit our site and dig deeper with our books into your area of interest: Quarto Creates, Quarto Cooks, Quarto Homes, Quarto Lives, Quarto Drives, Quarto Explores, Quarto Gifts, or Quarto Kids.

First Published in 2019 by Quarry Books, an imprint of The Quarto Group,
100 Cummings Center, Suite 265-D, Beverly, MA 01915, USA.
T (978) 282-9590 F (978) 283-2742 QuartoKnows.com

Quarry Books titles are also available at discount for retail, wholesale, promotional, and bulk purchase. For details, contact the Special Sales Manager by email at specialsales@quarto.com or by mail at The Quarto Group, Attn: Special Sales Manager, 100 Cummings Center, Suite 265-D, Beverly, MA 01915, USA.

10 9 8 7 6 5 4

ISBN: 978-0-7603-6256-3

Digital edition published in 2019
eISBN: 978-0-7603-6257-0

Library of Congress Cataloging-in-Publication Data

Names: Lennig, Melissa, author.
Title: Sticks and stones : a kid's guide to building and exploring in the
   great outdoors / Melissa Lennig.
Description: Beverly, MA : Quarry Books, an imprint of The Quarto Group,
   [2019] | Audience: Ages 8-13.
Identifiers: LCCN 2018051777 | ISBN 9780760362563 (flexi-bind)
Subjects: LCSH: Outdoor recreation for children. | Children and the
   environment.
Classification: LCC GV191.63 .L46 2019 | DDC 796.5083--dc23 LC record available at https://lccn.loc.
gov/2018051777

Book Design: Rita Sowins / Sowins Design
Cover Images: Melissa Lennig
Photography: Melissa Lennig

Printed in China

For my favorite outdoor adventurers Todd, Colin, and Owen

Contents

Section 1 / Create and Build with Logs ... 13

Section 2 / Sticks: The Original Wooden Toy ... 57

Section 3 / Easy Rock Projects 101

Introduction

Several years ago, my husband unexpectedly lost his job. Because his job included room and board, we lost our home too. Feeling hopeless and rather defeated, we packed almost all of our belongings—including our kids' toys and books—into a storage facility, then set route for my grandparents' cottage in rural New Hampshire.

Surrounded by decades-old sugar maple trees and crisp woodland air, our spirits lifted. I soon noticed that nature made us feel better, and it was also rich with creative art and building supplies. From sticks and stones to pine cones, my toddler and preschooler enjoyed an abundance of natural materials to play, create, and build with. They didn't even miss their toys!

Together we made bird feeders, raced bark boats, and engineered log forts in the woods. The kids scrabbled over boulders, jumped in leaf piles, explored sphagnum moss bogs, planted a garden, and raised tadpoles (and much to my chagrin, mosquito larvae) in an old aquarium.

This free, unstructured play in the forest suited my kids. As their resilience and physical strength increased, so did their self-confidence, creativity, and positive relationship with the environment. We began to make outdoor play a daily priority, through sun, rain, wind, and nor'easter. (Or as we called them in New Hampshire, "wicked big stahms!")

After some time, a new career brought my family to the growing suburbs of Columbus, Ohio. Though homes, thriving businesses, and two-lane streets now surround us, we still live by the motto, "Outdoor Play Everyday" and manage to find wild in city parks, public school yards, and even our own small backyard.

➡ How to Use This Book

Research shows that a daily dose of unstructured, outdoor play is essential for the physical and social-emotional health of kids. But the keyword there is **unstructured**. So let this book inspire play, not dictate it.

This book will introduce your family to thirty outdoor science, technology, engineering, art, and math (STEAM) projects that center around the use of sticks and stones.

Each activity includes a description, design challenge, list of materials, and an easy-to-understand explanation of the process. Many of the projects include enrichment activities designed to pique curiosity and inspire kids to develop more creative ideas of their own.

➡ Where to Play Outside

If you enjoyed a childhood teeming with outdoor free play, many of the activities in this book may feel familiar and bring back fond memories of days spent wandering the neighborhood with friends until the streetlights turned on.

But things are a *little* different in today's world. There are rules, regulations, safety concerns, and brilliantly lit screens that keep kids indoors and inhibit outdoor play.

The good news is that many nature centers, schools, and parks are recognizing that kids need outdoor areas to freely play, learn, and roam, and they are servicing that community need through the formation of **natural play areas.**

Natural play areas are outdoor spaces designated for off-trail exploring, building, and creeking. At natural play areas, kids can swim, dig, pick flowers, climb trees, stack rocks, build with logs, and collect toads, insects, and crayfish to their heart's content. Interacting with nature hands-on instills a vested sense of wonder and encourages kids to be responsible, caring stewards of the natural world.

➡ Embracing Risky Play

By definition, risky play is a play activity that involves the risk of physical injury. It's play that gives kids unique opportunities to test limits and master new challenges. Swinging, climbing, building, balancing, and jumping are just some of the risky play activities embraced in this book. Blend that with the idea of unstructured child-led outdoor play in all types of weather and you may be feeling new gray hairs pop!

The thing about kids is that they are capable. When given the opportunity, even very young children are able to manage risk and assess their own physical limitations.

We do have one ground rule though . . . mostly for the sake of my hair!

➡ Outdoor Play Ground Rule: Play Mindfully

Mindfulness, or the process of being fully present and aware, is an important social-emotional skill for kids to develop. Mindfulness gives kids space and time to pay attention to what is going on with their body, the environment, and other people around them. Here are some examples of how to apply this rule to outdoor play:

» Listen to your body. If you can't climb that tree all by yourself, you may not be ready yet.
» You found an awesome stick! Please be mindful of those around you as you play with it.
» We used cording to build a tripod. We need to be mindful of the environment and make sure all the cording comes home with us.

➡ Other Safety Considerations

Playing with sticks and stones is inherently risky business, but as you work through this book, you will notice several of the activities may also involve campfires, hand tools, a pocketknife, or water.

Adult supervision is recommended for these activities, and young children in particular should never be left unattended around fire, tools, knives, and water.

Other things to consider before you head outside?

» INSECTS (particularly ticks and mosquitoes): Take measures to protect yourself and your kids by wearing insect repellent. And be sure to cover skin when you are out in tick-infested areas.
» WEATHER: Encourage kids to stay hydrated by drinking plenty of water, protect skin from the sun by wearing sunscreen, and steer clear of playing outside during electrical storms.
» PLANTS: Learn how to identify and avoid poison ivy. Instruct your kids not to eat anything from the wild without adult permission.

➡ Final Thoughts

My own children and their friends worked through all thirty activities shared in this book. They giggled, got soaked with water, played in mud, created, built, and discovered!

I hope this book inspires your family to get outside and enjoy the hammering of woodpeckers, the cool rush of creek water, and the laughter of children as they enjoy, explore, and engineer the great outdoors. For no matter where you live, there is always an adventure to be had outside.

Create AND BUILD WITH Logs

From remarkable play forts to luxurious bug hotels, there is so much you can create and build with logs!

In this section, you'll engineer a log survival shelter (page 15), play with friends on a log seesaw while learning about simple machines (page 49), and invite birds to a backyard feast by building a rustic log bird feeder (page 36).

Please understand that none of the activities in this book require you to cut down living trees. All of the projects can be created with logs, sticks, and branches gathered from the forest floor.

Because of this, your finished projects may look different than ours. The diameter, length, and species of your logs may vary. That is perfectly okay! Get outside, be inspired, and enjoy creating and building with logs.

Build a Survival Shelter

→ In emergency situations, **a well-constructed survival shelter** built on dry land can be lifesaving! The purpose of a survival shelter is to protect your body from rain, wind, or snow. In the summer, a survival shelter can provide shade from the hot sun.

As a rule, your survival shelter should only be large enough to fit you and whoever else is with you. This is because large shelters are difficult to heat, and if you are in a survival situation, you want your shelter to keep your body heat where it belongs . . . close to you!

Materials

★ Fallen tree or large rock
★ Logs and branches
★ Natural materials, such as pine needles, sticks, moss, pine boughs, leaves, or bark

Safety Tips:

★ Assist small children with heavy logs.
★ For safety reasons, do not play inside of the shelter while it is in the process of being built.
★ Work gloves can help protect small hands.

fig. 1

fig. 2

fig. 3

STEP 1: After locating a fallen tree or large rock, begin stacking an angled wall of logs, sticks, and branches against it to build a lean-to. **(fig. 1)**

STEP 2: When the wall is complete, crawl into the lean-to and make sure it's long enough for your body. If necessary, increase the length of your lean-to by stacking more logs, sticks, and branches. **(fig. 2)**

STEP 3: Cover the wall of the lean-to with leaves, pine needles, pine boughs, moss, or bark from the forest floor. **(fig. 3)**

STEP 4: Create a thick bed of dry leaves or pine needles on the floor of your lean-to for comfort and warmth.

STEP 5: Your survival shelter is complete!

YOUR DESIGN CHALLENGE:

Build a basic survival shelter using logs, branches, sticks, and leaves.

Take It Further

» Using only the materials around you, can you create a survival shelter for two people? Three people?

» When the seasons change, experiment with building a winter survival shelter. What new seasonal material can you use in your building process?

Make an Emergency Survival Pack

Being prepared with an emergency survival pack can help you feel confident and in control during emergency situations. It's always smart to carry your survival pack on day trips, hikes, and camping adventures. Review all survival pack items with your grown-up to make sure you understand how to use them properly.

To make an emergency survival pack, prepare a backpack with the following:

» Gallon-size plastic bag for holding items and for water collection
» Water bottle
» Nonperishable food, such as protein bars and trail mix
» Travel-size first aid kit
» Lightweight flashlight, such as a headlamp
» Whistle to signal for help
» Mirror to signal for help
» Plastic rain poncho to stay dry and for shelter building
» Mylar emergency blanket

If you have permission from your adult, your emergency survival pack may also include rope, a pocketknife, and a magnesium fire starter or waterproof matches. It may also be comforting to pack insect repellent wipes, hard candies, and a small stuffed animal (for emotional support). If you are dependent upon any medications, such as an asthma inhaler, you may wish to pack that as well.

No kid ever expects to become lost or separated while enjoying the great outdoors. But just in case, you should know what to do.

1. Do not wander or hide; stay in one place.
2. If you are lost or separated with a friend, sibling, or pet, stay together.
3. Keep yourself warm and dry. If possible, wear bright clothes.
4. Attract attention by signaling for help with your whistle, mirror, and voice.

Making a Log Tripod

»»→ A tripod is a stable three-legged frame used for supporting the weight of another object. Perhaps you've seen or used a camera tripod. Building and using a log tripod is the same concept!

In the great outdoors, a basic tripod is a handy thing to have for cooking over a campfire, hanging a lantern, drying clothes, gardening, and fort building.

Materials

- ☆ **3 fallen branches or logs**
- ☆ **Cording, such as twine or parachute cord**
- ☆ **#16 jack chain (optional)**

Tools

- ☆ **Scissors or pocketknife**
- ☆ **Handsaw (optional)**

Safety Tips

- ☆ **Assist small children with heavy logs.**
- ☆ **Work gloves can help protect small hands.**
- ☆ **Do not leave your log tripod unattended over a lit campfire.**

Process

fig. 1

fig. 2

fig. 3

STEP 1: Locate 3 fallen branches or logs to be the poles of your tripod. The poles you choose should be of similar length and thickness. If needed, have an adult help you cut the poles to equal length with a handsaw.

STEP 2: Lay the three poles next to each other on the ground. Make a clove hitch (page 22) around one of the poles with the cording, cinching it tight. (fig. 1)

STEP 3: Lash the poles together by weaving the cording in and out of the three poles, creating five racking turns on each pole. (fig. 2)

STEP 4: When the racking is complete, pull the twine over the rope in between the poles for two frapping turns. (fig. 3)

STEP 5: Finish the process by making a clove hitch on the same pole you began with. Cut off any excess cording with your scissors or pocketknife.

STEP 6: Stand the poles upright and pull them apart to open the tripod. (fig. 4)

STEP 7: Your tripod is complete! If desired, secure a length of #16 jack chain from the center of the tripod so you can hang a pot for outdoor cooking.

fig. 4

Build a functional tripod
with logs and cording.

Take It Further

» Build a small tripod, and then see
if you can figure out how to turn it
into a stool.
» Grow pole beans along the poles
of your tripod.
» Drape a blanket or rain poncho
over the tripod to make a quick
and easy shelter or play fort.

How to Make a Clove Hitch

Follow along with the images above
to learn how to make a clove hitch.

Pendulum Painting with a Tripod

A pendulum is an object or weight hung from a point that enables it to swing back and forth due to the force of gravity.

In this activity, learn about the forces of gravity, motion, and friction by creating colorful pendulum art with your log tripod.

Materials

- ☆ Tempera paint
- ☆ Water
- ☆ Empty jars, such as mason jars
- ☆ Log tripod
- ☆ Extra-large paper
- ☆ Stones
- ☆ Single hole punch
- ☆ Compostable plastic cup
- ☆ Phillips-head screwdriver
- ☆ Cording, such as twine or parachute cord
- ☆ Pocketknife or scissors

STEP 1: Prepare the tempera paints in empty containers by mixing one part paint with one part water.

STEP 2: Pull the tripod open over grass and then lay one sheet of paper directly below it. Place a small stone on each corner of the paper so it doesn't blow away.

STEP 3: Prepare the pendulum by using the single hole punch to create one hole on each side of the cup. Next, twist the Phillips-head screwdriver through the plastic to create a hole in the bottom of the cup. Tie a piece of cording through the holes on the side of the cup.

STEP 4: Cut a length of cording that is the same length as the poles of your tripod. Fold the end and tie a knot to create a loop. Place the loop over the middle pole of your tripod.

STEP 5: Next, tie the end of the looped cording to the center of the cording on the plastic cup. Before securing your knot, adjust the length of the looped cording, being sure the cup has space to swing back and forth over the paper. Use a pocketknife or scissors to remove any extra cording.

STEP 6: Pull the cup back, place a finger over the hole, and pour your prepared tempera paint into the cup.

STEP 7: Let go of the cup! Observe the designs the pendulum makes as it swings back and forth and around the paper.

STEP 8: Allow your paintings to dry flat on the ground. Repeat steps 6 and 7 to create more incredible art with science!

Construct a Handy Travois

▶▶→ If you are playing outside and ever come across a rock or log that is too heavy to carry, a travois can help you move it! **A travois (pronounced "trav-oy")** is a Native American drag sled that was traditionally pulled by dogs or horses to carry heavy loads on land.

The travois you build for outdoor play will be a handy tool for pulling building supplies, backpacks, and little brothers or sisters over flat trails!

Materials

★ **2 long branches or logs that resemble poles**
★ **Branches or logs to use as crosspieces**
★ **Cording, such as twine or parachute cord**

Tools

★ **Handsaw (optional)**
★ **Scissors or pocketknife**

Safety Tips

★ **Assist small children with heavy logs.**
★ **Work gloves can help protect small hands.**
★ **Wear eye protection while using tools.**
★ **Do not pull your travois over rocky or bumpy land.**

fig. 1

fig. 2

Take It Further

» What changes can you make to your design to build a travois for two people to pull?

» Build a second travois, but make the base on the drag end more narrow. Is the travois harder or easier to pull? Why?

» A travois is a type of simple machine called a second-class lever. Can you locate the load, fulcrum, and effort?

STEP 1: Locate 2 fallen branches or logs to be the poles of your travois. The poles you choose should be of similar length and thickness. If needed, have an adult help you cut the poles to equal length with a handsaw.

STEP 2: Lay the poles so that the two thinner ends overlap forming the shape of an X. These overlapping poles will be the handles of your travois. (fig. 1)

STEP 3: Tie a clove hitch (page 22) around one of the poles with the cording, cinching it tight.

STEP 4: Weave the twine around the two poles until they are firmly in place. (fig. 2)

STEP 5: When the lashing (weaving) is complete, pull the twine over the rope in between the poles for two frapping turns.

STEP 6: Position a crosspiece in the upper 1/3 of the frame so that the travois looks similar to a letter A. Lash the crosspiece to the frame of the travois with cording. (fig. 3)

STEP 7: Repeat step 6 with as many crosspieces as you would like to use.

STEP 8: Your travois is complete and ready for transporting heavy loads. (fig. 4)

fig. 4

fig. 3

Construct a functional travois with logs and cording.

A Hotel for Bugs

»→ Building a bug hotel is an easy and fun way to invite beneficial insects like solitary bees, ladybugs, and lacewings into your garden. Once settled, your new six-legged-friends will happily pollinate your fruits and vegetables, and they'll help control unwanted garden pests such as aphids.

Using a premade wooden CD crate from your local craft store and a variety of natural materials including logs, sticks, and pine cones, you can make your bug hotel an inviting and welcoming place for helpful insects to live, lay eggs, and gather.

Materials

- ☆ 1 small premade wooden CD crate
- ☆ Self-sealing acrylic paint (also known as outdoor acrylic paint)
- ☆ Paintbrush (optional)
- ☆ 3 log pillars
- ☆ Natural materials, such as sticks, pine cones, moss, lichens, and dry leaves

Tools

- ☆ Handsaw
- ☆ Cordless drill
- ☆ ¼-inch drill bit

Safety Tips

- ☆ Adult supervision is recommended during activities requiring tools.
- ☆ Work gloves can help protect small hands.
- ☆ Wear eye protection while using tools.

fig. 1

YOUR DESIGN CHALLENGE:

Use craft supplies, logs, and other natural materials to build a hotel for bugs.

STEP 1: If desired, paint both the inside and outside of the CD crate with outdoor acrylic paint. **(fig. 1)**

TIP: If you don't wish to use acrylic paint, try staining the CD crate with DIY ochre paint (page 134).

STEP 2: While the paint is drying, ask an adult to help you cut the log pillars so they fit inside of the CD crate. We cut our log pillars to a length of about 4 inches (10 cm), leaving the bark intact. **(fig. 2)**

STEP 3: Ask an adult to help you drill holes in your log pillars with a cordless drill. Solitary leafcutter bees prefer holes that are ¼-inch (6 mm) wide and about 3 inches (7.5 cm) deep. **(fig. 3)**

STEP 4: When the log pillars are finished, stack them inside of the CD crate.

STEP 5: Fill in the gaps around your pillars with bundles of sticks, pine cones, leaves, moss, and lichens.

STEP 6: Your bug hotel is complete! Place the finished bug hotel near your garden, and enjoy observing the insects that make it home.

DID YOU KNOW?

Ladybugs can eat about seventy-five aphids in a single day, so inviting them to stay at your bug hotel will help keep your plants happy and healthy!

fig. 3

fi. 4

Magical Play Fort

»→ Fort building provides opportunities to develop engineering skills while simultaneously flexing problem-solving, communication, and teamwork skills.

Growing up, my brothers and I built log forts all throughout the woods that surrounded our home. They were the perfect place for reading, dreaming, and playing with friends.

If you've successfully built a log tripod, then building a magical play fort will be a simple and fun experience, as you will use a tripod as the frame of the fort. Vibrant silk scarves draped over the logs make the fort feel cozy, magical, and made just for kids!

Materials

☆ **Logs**
☆ **Cording, such as twine or parachute cord**
☆ **Silk scarves, in a variety of colors**

Tools

☆ **Scissors or pocketknife**

Safety Tips

☆ **Assist small children with heavy logs.**
☆ **Work gloves can help protect small hands.**
☆ **For safety reasons, do not play in the fort while it is in the process of being built.**

fig. 1

fig. 2

fig. 3

STEP 1: Use the process from Project 2: Make a Log Tripod (page 18) to build the frame of your fort. (fig. 1)

STEP 2: After the tripod is complete, carefully lean more logs against it. (fig. 2)

To balance the weight on the tripod, we found it best to place new logs in a symmetrical fashion. We ended up using a total of ten logs, but you may wish to use more . . . or less! (fig. 3)

STEP 3: Drape colorful silk scarves over the logs. Silk is well suited for outdoor play because soft light can shine through the fabric, leaving your fort feeling bright and playful. (fig. 4) (fig. 5)

TIP: If you don't have silk scarves, light cotton bed sheets, ribbons, or sheer curtains can provide a similar effect.

STEP 4: Your magical play fort is complete! Enjoy relaxing inside of it with friends.

YOUR DESIGN CHALLENGE:

Build a tripod-frame play fort with logs, silk scarves, and cording.

fig. 4

fig. 5

DIY Log Bird Feeders

▶▶→ If there is one thing I could happily do all day long,
it's observing birds. I love to watch them flit about in the branches
and around the bird feeder. So do my kids!

This DIY Log Bird Feeder is simple and fun to make.
My Dad fondly calls them "Peanut Butter Logs," as he likes to stuff the holes of the
feeder with a mixture of natural peanut butter, birdseed, and cornmeal to attract
woodpeckers, chickadees, and nuthatches.

If you don't wish to use homemade peanut butter
and birdseed mixture, you can also stuff the holes with store-bought suet.
Look for suet in the same aisle as birdseed.

Materials

* ★ 1 log with bark intact
* ★ 1 screw-in hook
* ★ Homemade peanut butter birdseed mixture or suet
* ★ Spoon
* ★ 1 branch hook
* ★ Empty storage container

Tools

* ★ Handsaw
* ★ Cordless drill
* ★ 1-inch spade drill bit
* ★ 8/32 inch drill bit

Safety Tips

* ★ Assist small children with heavy logs.
* ★ Work gloves can help protect small hands.
* ★ Wear eye protection while using tools.

fig. 1

fig. 2

fig. 3

STEP 1: Part of the fun of this project is getting outside to choose your log. Try to choose a firm, healthy log that boasts beautiful, rough bark.

The log you choose should be 4- to 5-inches (10 to 13 cm) in diameter. Have an adult help you cut it with a handsaw to a length of about 12 inches (30 cm).

STEP 2: Ask an adult to help you drill 1-inch (2.5-cm) holes, approximately 1½ inches (3.5 cm) deep, all throughout the log. **(fig. 1)**

STEP 3: Use an $8/32$ inch drill bit to start a small hole at the top of the log for your screw-in hook.

STEP 4: Secure the screw-in hook to the top of the bird feeder. **(fig. 2)**

YOUR DESIGN CHALLENGE:

Build and maintain a log bird feeder to attract wild birds.

STEP 5: Use a spoon or your fingers to fill the holes of the bird feeder with homemade peanut butter birdseed mixture or suet. **(fig.3)**

STEP 6: Your log bird feeder is complete! Hang it on a branch hook near your favorite bird watching spot, and then keep a record of all the birds that visit.

Take It Further

» Does the type of log you choose for your bird feeder affect the variety of birds that will visit your feeder? Make a second feeder using a different kind of log. Hang them near each other and see which birds prefers each feeder.
» Maintain your bird feeder through all four seasons. Keep a record of the birds that visit each month.

How to Make Homemade Peanut Butter Birdseed

Birds that like to eat suet will happily enjoy a feast of homemade peanut butter birdseed.

INGREDIENTS
» 1/2 cup (130 g) natural peanut butter
» 1/2 cup (70 g) cornmeal
» 1/2 cup (weight will vary) birdseed

DIRECTIONS
1. Mix all of the ingredients together in an empty container with a spoon or your fingers.
2. Use your fingers or a spoon to fill the holes of the bird feeder.
3. Store unused peanut butter birdseed in a closed container in a cool, dry location until it's time to refill the log bird feeder.

I promise, step 3 won't take very long! Especially if any hungry squirrels manage to find your feeder!

Log Weaving Loom Fort

»→ Weaving is one of the oldest crafts in the world.
Dating back to ancient times, weaving was used to create shelters,
baskets, and fences out of logs and branches.

In the forest or backyard, an outdoor weaving loom is a creative way to combine
outdoor play with art. Made from logs, cording, and other natural materials,
the loom is a fun place to experiment with texture and color while developing
engineering skills, fine-motor skills, and mindfulness.

Materials

☆ **7 logs of equal length and thickness**
☆ **Cording, such as twine or parachute cord**
☆ **Silk scarves, in a variety of colors**
☆ **Natural materials, such as leaves, grasses, ferns, flowers, feathers, and sticks**

Tools

☆ **Handsaw**
☆ **Scissors or pocketknife**

Safety Tips

☆ **Assist small children with heavy logs.**
☆ **Work gloves can help protect small hands.**
☆ **Wear eye protection while using tools.**

fig. 1

fig. 2

Take It Further

Plant pole beans, clematis vine, or sweet peas along the foundation of your fort. Observe as the plants naturally weave through the cording as they grow and have fun playing in your "living" fort!

STEP 1: Gather seven logs of equal length and thickness. If necessary, ask an adult to help you cut the logs to equal length with a handsaw.

STEP 2: Lay two of the logs side by side with the top ends crossed in the shape of an X. Lash the logs together with cording, then set them aside.

STEP 3: Repeat step 2 with two more logs.

TIP: Enlist the help of a friend, sibling, or grown-up for step 4. It's definitely a job for two people!

STEP 4: Stand up the logs with the crossed ends pointing up. Next, place the fifth log on top of the lashed logs, balancing it in the crevice where the logs cross. Lash the "ridge" log to the others with cording. **(fig. 1)**

After completing this step, the frame should be able to stand on its own.

STEP 5: Now you are going to see your A-frame weaving loom fort come together! Lash the sixth and seventh logs (your support logs) to the bottom sides of the fort with cording.

Build an A-frame weaving loom fort with logs, cording, and a variety of other natural materials.

STEP 6: To stabilize the frame, tie a length of cording in a diagonal fashion from the top right corner to the bottom left corner of each side of the frame.

STEP 7: Prepare the fort for weaving by tying cording over the "ridge" log, then running it down to the bottom "support" log where you will tie it off. (fig. 2)

STEP 8: Continue tying the twine equally along both sides of the frame.

STEP 9: Weave silk scarves, leaves, grasses, ferns, flowers, feathers, and sticks along the frame.

STEP 10: Your log weaving loom fort is complete! Enjoy playing in your fort with friends. (fig. 3)

fig. 3

Log Walking Blocks

▶▶→ Have you ever wished to be just a little bit taller?
Walking blocks are a form of stilts for kids. They are fun for
outdoor picnics and parties and make a thoughtful homemade gift.

Choose strong, firm logs for your walking blocks. Our pair of sturdy birch
walking blocks was about 6 inches (15 cm) high. If you are making walking blocks
for a small child, you may wish to cut your logs to a length of 3 inches (7.5 cm).

Materials

★ **Two 3- to 6-inch (7.5- to
  15-cm) log pillars that
  measure about 4 inches
  (10 cm) across the top**
★ **Cording, such as twine
  or parachute cord**

Tools

★ **Handsaw**
★ **½-inch drill bit**
★ **Cordless drill**
★ **Scissors or pocketknife**

Safety Tips

★ **Work gloves can help
  protect small hands.**
★ **Wear eye protection while
  using tools.**
★ **Avoid using your pair of
  log walking blocks on
  hard or slippery surfaces.
  Grass is best!**

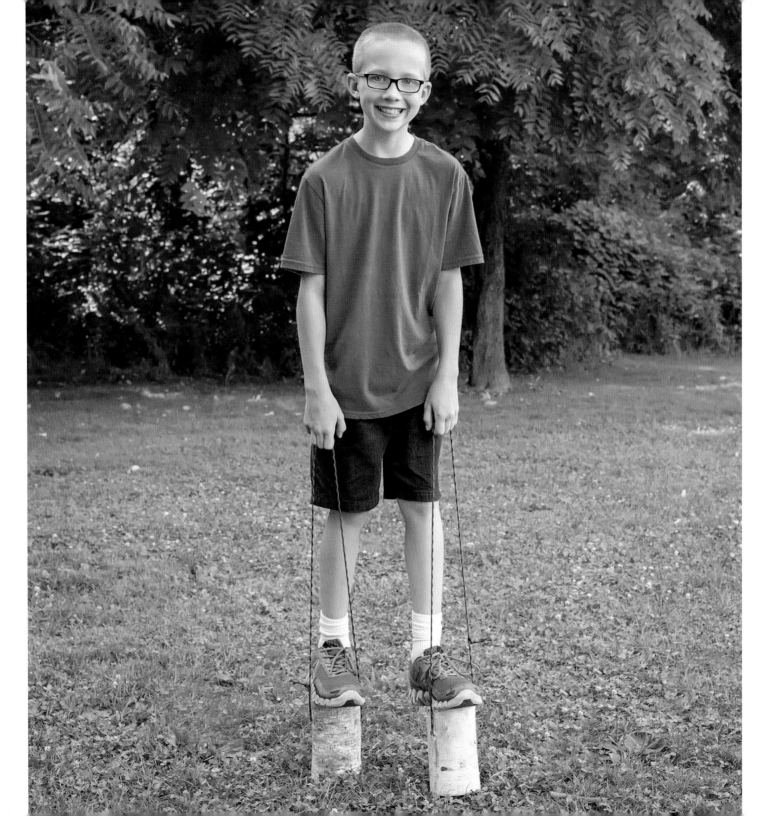

fig. 1

fig. 2

fig. 3

STEP 1: Ask an adult to help you cut the log pillars to your desired length with a handsaw. We found 3 to 6 inches (7.5 to 15 cm) to be a safe length for most kids. **(fig. 1)**

STEP 2: Ask an adult to help you use a cordless drill fitted with a ½-inch drill bit to drill a hole completely through the side of the log. We placed our hole about 2 inches (5 cm) down from the top of the log. **(fig. 2)**

STEP 3: Thread 2 feet (60 cm) of cording through each log pillar and then tie it off. Remove excess cording with a pocketknife or scissors. **(fig. 3 and fig. 4)**

STEP 4: Your log walking blocks are complete! Carefully stand on them, pull up the cording, and enjoy the challenge of coordinating your arms and legs while you walk on the blocks around your yard.

fig. 4

Build a pair of walking blocks from log pillars and cording.

Take It Further

» Create walking-block art by stepping into washable paint with the walking blocks, then stamping a fresh sheet of paper.
» Count how many steps you can take on your walking blocks before toppling over. Keep a tally of your results!
» Challenge friends, siblings, and grown-ups to a walking-block relay race.

A Simple Seesaw

➡➡ Let nature be your playground! Making a seesaw from logs is so much fun. While you lift up, your friend goes down . . . but how does it work?

A seesaw is a type of simple machine called a lever. Simple machines, like levers, are designed to simplify work. Levers, which reduce the amount of force needed to lift and move objects, have four parts:

1. BAR: This is the part of the seesaw you sit on.

2. FULCRUM: This is the part of the seesaw that the bar pivots on.

3. EFFORT: This is the force you apply to move the bar. When you seesaw, you create force by bending your knees and pushing off the ground.

4. LOAD: The load is the object you are trying to move or lift.

Materials

★ 2 logs

Safety Tips

★ Assist small children with heavy logs.
★ Work gloves can help protect small hands.

fig. 1

fig. 2

YOUR DESIGN CHALLENGE:

Using only logs, build a
simple seesaw.

Take It Further

» What other kind of playground equipment can you make with logs? Build a small nature playground for you and your friends to enjoy.
» How does using a shorter bar change the movement of your seesaw?
» Work with your partner to balance the bar of the seesaw. What do you need to adjust to make it work?

STEP 1: Work with a partner to position one long log (the bar) on top of a shorter log (the fulcrum). (fig. 1 and fig. 2)

STEP 2: Your log seesaw is finished! Invite a friend to sit opposite you on the bar of the seesaw and have fun playing together.

Log Easel
for Little Artists

➤➤➤ From wispy cloud formations in the sky to a rainbow of colors in the garden, nature is full of inspiration and a **muse for young artists.** Make sketching and painting outside easy and fun with a rustic log easel. It's perfect for backyards!

The special thing about this tripod easel is that it folds up for convenient storage. We recommend only using the log easel on grass so that it doesn't wiggle or move while you paint.

Materials

- ☆ **3 long logs of equal length (about 45 inches or 114 cm)**
- ☆ **1 small log (about 22 inches or 56 cm)**
- ☆ **1-inch drill bit**
- ☆ **1 stick**
- ☆ **Cording, such as twine or parachute cord**
- ☆ **Tempera paint**
- ☆ **Canvas squares**
- ☆ **Paintbrushes**

Tools

- ☆ **Handsaw**
- ☆ **Scissors or pocketknife**

Safety Tips

- ☆ **Assist small children with heavy logs.**
- ☆ **Work gloves can help protect small hands.**
- ☆ **Wear eye protection while using tools.**

fig. 1

fig. 2

fig. 3

STEP 1: Have an adult help you cut three logs to a length of about 45 inches (114 cm). Lay the logs down on the ground side by side.

STEP 2: Ask an adult to help you drill a 1-inch (2.5-cm) hole through the top of each log with a cordless drill. We drilled our holes about 3 inches (7.5 cm) down from the top. **(fig. 1)**

STEP 3: Slide the stick through the hole in each log, connecting them together. **(fig. 2)**

STEP 4: Stand up the logs, then separate the legs of the easel by pushing the middle log back. The easel should stand upright on its own. **(fig. 3)**

STEP 5: Tie a small log to the front of the easel with cording. This is the part of the easel your canvas will rest on. Remove excess twine with scissors or a pocketknife. **(fig. 4)**

DID YOU KNOW?
People have been using easels for painting since the time of the ancient Egyptians!

STEP 6: Your easel is complete! Enjoy painting and creating outdoors. **(fig. 5)**

YOUR DESIGN CHALLENGE:

Design and build a folding log easel.

fig. 4

Take It Further

Use the easel to display finished artwork or signs.

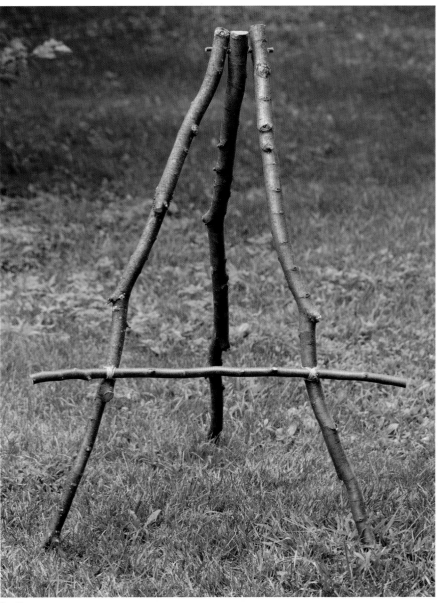

fig. 5

When my dog, Thatcher, is given the choice between a store-bought toy or a stick, hands-down, he will choose the stick each time.

Thatcher is definitely on to something! From helpful tools to fun toys, there is so much to make and do with sticks.

In this section, you'll learn how to make a functional stick fishing pole (page 71), engineer a rustic stick catapult (page 93), and amaze your friends with DIY stick bubble wands and our top-secret monster bubble formula (page 63).

So get outdoors and start collecting sticks from your yard, the park, and your neighborhood. Sure, you may look weird hauling bundles of sticks around town, but like Thatcher, you know where the **real** fun is!

Guess What . . .
While writing and photographing the activities for this book, Thatcher was a master photobomber and stick thief!

Once, while taking a break in between photo sessions, Thatcher crept up to the supply bin and grabbed all four of our Roasting sticks (page 85) at once. The kids ran after him to get then sticks back, but Thatcher was too fast! With a wagging tail and a satisfied grin, Thatcher laid down under an oak tree to chew the marshmallow-coated cooking sticks.

Section 2

Sticks: THE ORIGINAL Wooden TOY

Stick Boat Races

>>→ Building stick boats and racing them down a bubbling creek is fun way to relax and play when the weather is warm.

When my kids were preschoolers, they enjoyed floating milkweed pod boats in muddy puddles on the dirt road near our house. With a little imagination and resourcefulness, just about any natural material that floats can become a toy boat.

Materials

- ☆ **5–10 pencil-length sticks**
- ☆ **Cording, such as twine or parachute cord**
- ☆ **Fresh leaves**
- ☆ **Single hole paper punch (optional)**
- ☆ **Hot glue (optional)**
- ☆ **Tape (optional)**

Tools

- ☆ **Pruning shears (optional)**
- ☆ **Pocketknife or scissors**

Safety Tips:

- ☆ **Only adults should use pruning shears.**
- ☆ **Adult supervision is recommended during water activities.**

fig. 1

fig. 2

STEP 1: Gather and arrange 5 to 10 pencil-length sticks in a row. You may need to break the sticks or ask an adult to cut them to equal length with a pair of pruning shears.

STEP 2: Use a clove hitch (see page 22) to secure a 1-yard (91 cm) piece of cording to the outer left stick.

TIP: If your sticks are thicker than a pencil, you may need more cording.

STEP 3: Pick up the second stick and place it on top of the twine, next to the first stick. **(fig. 1)**

STEP 4: Pull the twine around and over the top of the second stick, and then wrap it around the bottom of the first stick. Next, pull the twine over the top of the first stick, and then pull it under the second stick.

When you are finished, the twine should be in the shape of the number eight.

STEP 5: Repeat in this fashion until all of the sticks are lashed together

STEP 6: Weave the tail end of the twine back through the sticks, being sure to wrap it around the twine already in place (racking turns). This will secure the twine and prevent it from slipping off the boat.

STEP 7: Secure the end of the twine with a clove hitch or tie it off with a tight knot.

STEP 8: Repeat steps 2–7 on the opposite side of the boat.

STEP 9: Secure a mast to the toy boat by wedging a stick upright in the center. If desired, secure the stick to the boat with a small squeeze of hot glue.

STEP 10: Poke a leaf through the mast to give the stick boat a sail. **(fig. 2)**

We've found that using a single hole paper punch to create two holes in the leaf helps to keep the leaf from tearing. If desired, secure the leaf sail to the mast of the boat with a small piece of tape.

STEP 11: Your stick boat is complete! Enjoy racing your boat down creeks and streams with friends. **(fig. 3)**

fig. 3

YOUR DESIGN CHALLENGE:

Construct a functional toy boat from sticks, cording, and other natural materials.

Take It Further

» After sailing your boat, challenge it with weight by placing small stones on top of it. How many stones can your boat carry? What can you do to make it hold more stones?

» Follow your boat down the creek or stream. Observe where it gets stuck, when it moves quickly, or where it slows down. What is going on in the environment that causes this to happen?

» No cording? See if you can create a boat with a log, bark, pine cones, or seedpods.

Bubble Wands

➤➤→ Is there anything more magical than a cloud of **shimmering bubbles floating** toward the sky? I don't think so! Bubbles can liven up parties and events and bust boredom like no toy can!

Over the years, my kids and I have created and tested several homemade bubble solutions. Our favorite solution produces strong, lofty bubbles that float high above the roof of our home.

Paired with DIY stick bubble wands, you too can amaze your friends with gigantic MONSTER bubbles!

Materials
☆ **Two 12-inch (30-cm) sticks**
☆ **Cotton yarn**
☆ **2 #10 screw hooks**
☆ **1 metal washer**

Tools
☆ **Pruning shears (optional)**
☆ **Pocketknife or scissors**

Safety Tips
☆ **Only adults should use pruning shears.**
☆ **Wear eye protection while mixing your bubble solution.**

fig. 1

fig. 2

STEP 1: Gather two 12-inch (30-cm) sticks. You may need to break the sticks or ask an adult to cut them to equal length with a pair of pruning shears.

STEP 2: Twist 1 #10 screw hook into the end of each stick. (fig. 1)

STEP 3: Cut two lengths of cotton yarn. One string should measure about 60 inches (152 cm) long while the other string should measure about 30 inches (76 cm) long.

STEP 4: Tie the ends of both strings onto the screw hook of one stick.

STEP 5: String the metal washer through the 30-inch (76-cm) piece of yarn.

STEP 6: Tie the remaining loose ends of both strings onto the screw hook of the second stick. (fig. 2)

STEP 7: Your stick bubble wand is complete! To create bubbles, dip the strings of your bubble wand into bubble solution, and then gently pull the sticks through the air.

YOUR DESIGN CHALLENGE:

Craft rustic bubble wands from backyard sticks, yarn, and basic hardware supplies.

Homemade Bubble Solution Recipe

Making homemade bubble solution is easy and fun! You will need:

INGREDIENTS
» 4 cups (940 ml) distilled water
» 1 cup (235 ml) regular (not ultra) dish soap
» ¼ cup (60 ml) liquid glycerin

DIRECTIONS
Pour all of the ingredients into a large bowl and stir it well. For best results, allow the bubble solution to rest for 24 hours before using.

Take It Further

» Make colored bubbles by adding twenty drops of food coloring to your bubble solution.
» Make additional bubble wands. Experiment with lengthening or shortening the cotton yarn. What happens?
» Can cold winter air freeze a monster bubble? Try and see!

Small World in a Log Cabin

»→ Have you ever traipsed around the woods,
pretending to be a settler on the great frontier?

Long ago when pioneers settled on new land, one of the first things they
needed to do was build a home for their family. Using just an ax and the natural
materials around them, many pioneers built small log cabins.

Using modeling clay, sticks, and the same concept as early settlers, you too can
build your very own log cabin. Enjoy decorating your log cabin small world with
moss, stones, and plastic miniatures. It's perfect for imaginative play!

Materials

- ☆ **1 round wooden plaque**
- ☆ **Green acrylic paint**
- ☆ **Paintbrush**
- ☆ **25 sticks of equal size**
- ☆ **Modeling clay**
- ☆ **Natural materials, such as moss, stones, and bark**
- ☆ **Pioneer-inspired plastic miniatures**

Tools

- ☆ **Pruning shears (optional)**

Safety Tips

- ☆ **Only adults should use pruning shears.**

fig. 1

fig. 2

fig. 3

STEP 1: Paint the surface of the round wooden plaque green. (fig. 1)

STEP 2: While the paint is drying, go outside and collect about twenty-five sticks of equal size. You may need to break the sticks or ask an adult to cut them to equal length with a pair of pruning shears.

STEP 3: Begin stacking the sticks on the wooden plaque, log cabin style. Instead of notching each stick like the pioneers did their logs, use modeling clay to help your sticks fit together. (fig. 2)

STEP 4: Continue building until your log cabin is tall enough. (fig. 3)

STEP 5: Decorate the rest of your wooden plaque with stones, bark, and plastic miniatures. If desired, seal the cracks in your log cabin with modeling clay, mud, or air-dry clay.

STEP 6: Your log cabin small world is complete!

YOUR DESIGN CHALLENGE:

Create a log cabin small world scene with sticks, basic craft supplies, and natural materials.

Take It Further

» Invite a friend to build a large-scale log cabin with you outside.
» Instead of using modeling clay in this activity, collect natural clay from a creek bed or riverbank.

Classic Stick Fishing Pole

▶▶→ I once asked my son, "What do you like most about fishing with Grandpa?"

He simply replied, "I just like being there."

I thought about pressing for more details. Did he like the water?
The warm sun? The snacks? Then I realized by saying, **"I just like being there,"** he meant *all* of those things and more.

Fishing will teach you valuable social-emotional skills like patience and perseverance, and you will also learn how to be fully present with nature and other people. From choosing a quiet fishing hole to waiting for a fish to bite, it's the process of fishing that hooks you.

Catching a fish is just the bonus!

Process

Materials

- 1 stick with an approximate length of 1 yard (91 cm)
- 6–8 lb. test (breaking strength) fishing line
- 1 small snap swivel
- 1 size 6, 7, or 8 snell fish hook
- 1 small red and white bobber
- Live bait or assorted fishing lures

Tools

- Pocketknife or scissors
- Pruning shears (optional)
- Needle-nose pliers

YOUR DESIGN CHALLENGE:

Make a usable fishing pole from a stick and basic fishing supplies.

Safety Tips

- Only adults should use pruning shears.
- Use caution while tying and baiting hooks.
- Adult supervision is recommended during water activities.

STEP 1: Collect a stick from the forest floor that measures approximately 1 yard (91 cm) in length. Ask your grown-up to help you remove branches and twigs from the stick with a pocketknife or pruning shears. (fig. 1)

STEP 2: Unravel 5 inches (13 cm) of fishing line from the spool. Tie the fishing line to the thick handle end of your stick with a double knot.

STEP 3: Wind the fishing line around the stick all the way to the tip by twisting the stick with your wrist.

STEP 4: Secure the fishing line to the tip of the stick with a half hitch knot.

STEP 5: Use a pocketknife to cut a small split on the tip of your stick. Slide the hanging fishing line through the split.

STEP 6: Grasp the hanging line with your fingers and then pull it back down the stick to the handle. Cut the line free from the spool with scissors or a pocketknife.

STEP 7: Tie the line to the eye end of the small snap swivel with a clinch knot. Remove any excess line with scissors or a pocketknife. (fig. 2)

STEP 8: Place the line end of the snell fish hook through the clip end of the snap swivel. (fig. 3)

DID YOU KNOW?
People have enjoyed bait fishing with stick poles since ancient times. Early fishing hooks were often made from wood, bone, or shells.

STEP 9: Clip the bobber onto the fishing line 2 to 3 feet (61 to 91 cm) from the hook.

fig. 1

fig. 3

fig. 2

fig. 4

fig. 5

STEP 10: Your classic stick fishing pole is complete! Bait the hook with a worm or lure and then toss the line into the water. (fig. 4)

If you catch a fish, pull your line in quickly and smoothly. Ask an adult to help you remove the hook from the fish by grasping and then twisting the hook out with needle-nose pliers. Gently release the fish back into the water. (fig. 5)

TIP: When you are finished fishing, wind the line back toward the handle of your pole. Press the point of the hook into the pole until it is secured.

Take It Further

» Keep a journal of your fishing adventures! When you catch a fish, record the date, location, time of day, name of the fish, and its length. If desired, add a photograph or sketch of the fish.

» Experiment with different kinds of bait. Some fish even enjoy a thick ball of bread and peanut butter!

» Host a fishing tournament for your siblings and friends. The winning fisherman or fisherwoman takes home the coveted Golden Stick Fishing Pole! To make one, simply paint a stick with gold acrylic paint, seal it with clear spray sealer, and then follow steps 2–9 of the stick fishing pole process.

How to Make a Clinch Knot

Follow along with the images above to learn how to make a clinch knot.

Simple Stick Fence

»→ Since early times, people have built fences out of wood or stone to mark property and protect their homes, animals, and crops.

My family's crops (okay, our very small vegetable garden) definitely could use a fence. Something—most likely a rabbit or groundhog— has been munching our carrot greens!

In this activity, you will learn how to make a simple fence from sticks and cording. It's the perfect way to enclose your play area (or, as my kids like to call it, their "base"), protect your veggie patch, or mark trails and boundaries.

Materials

* Sticks, in a variety of sizes
* 1 round rock, about the size of your fist
* Cording, such as twine or parachute cord
* Scissors or a pocketknife

YOUR DESIGN CHALLENGE:

After gathering sticks in a variety of sizes, design and build a simple stick fence.

fig. 1

fig. 2

STEP 1: Choose the location, purpose, and size of your fence.

STEP 2: Gather sticks in a variety of sizes. You will need to collect thick sticks to use as fence posts, as well as smaller sticks and branches to drop between the fence posts.

STEP 3: Use a rock to pound the thick sticks—your fence posts—into the ground. Working in a row, space the fence posts 6 to 12 inches (15 to 30 cm) apart. **(fig. 1)**

STEP 4: Repeat on the opposite side, placing the new posts about 5 inches (13 cm) across from the initial row.

STEP 5: When the fence posts are secure in the ground, begin dropping smaller sticks and branches between the posts. **(fig. 2)**

STEP 6: To strengthen your fence and contain the sticks, tie opposite fence posts together with cording. **(fig. 3)**

STEP 7: Your simple stick fence is complete!

Take It Further

» Weave plants, such as ferns, leaves, and flowers, through your stick fence to camouflage it.

» Use trees as your fence posts instead of sticks.

fig. 3

Nature Blocks

▶▶→ Homemade nature blocks are easy to make and fun to play with. Use a handsaw to cut flat "tree pancakes" and one-of-a-kind blocks that are small enough to stack, build, and create with.

Additional natural objects such as pine cones, mosses, flowers, twigs, and stones can serve as a creative "expansion pack" for your new nature block set.

We keep our nature blocks outside under a tree, but they are also a great inside toy. Such a simple way to bring the great outdoors in!

Materials

☆ **Logs, sticks, and branches, in a variety of sizes and colors**
☆ **Natural materials, such as pinecones, moss, flowers, and bark**
☆ **Miniature fairies, gnomes, and animals (optional)**

Tools

☆ **Handsaw**
☆ **Sandpaper (optional)**

Safety Tips

☆ **Work gloves can help protect small hands.**
☆ **Adult supervision is recommended.**
☆ **Wear eye protection while using tools and sandpaper.**

fig. 1

fig. 2

fig. 3

STEP 1: Gather a variety of dry sticks and branches that have a diameter of 1 to 3 inches (2.5 to 7.5 cm). You may also enjoy collecting several thick logs that have a diameter of 5 to 7 inches (13 to 18 cm).

Don't forget about branches that are Y-shaped . . . they provide a creative building challenge!

STEP 2: Ask an adult to help you cut the branches, sticks, and logs with a handsaw. (fig. 1)

STEP 3: Continue, cutting the branches and sticks in a variety of sizes and shapes. (fig. 2)

STEP 4: When the blocks are cut, smooth any rough edges with sandpaper.

STEP 5: Your nature blocks are complete! Enjoy creating and building inside or outside with them. (fig. 3)

Take It Further

» Turn your block creations into a work of art by challenging yourself to build arches that appear to defy gravity.
» Use small, flat "tree cookies" to build staircases.
» Dye your nature blocks with liquid watercolors.

The Power of Blocks

Building with blocks not only enhances creativity and imagination, but also boasts many social-emotional and cognitive benefits as well.

As you build and create with friends or siblings, you are communicating ideas, learning to share, respecting each other's work, and developing problem-solving, math, and engineering skills. Some research has even shown that when kids play with blocks, they improve their visual-spatial skills and literacy skills.

Roasting Stick for Outdoor Cooking

▶▶→ There is something incredibly special about gathering with friends and family to **roast hot dogs** and **gooey marshmallows** over an open campfire. Sure, you can buy manufactured roasting sticks from the store, but why not make your own? It's easy, inexpensive, and a great way to get outside.

My oldest son loves to search the forest floor for forked sticks so he can roast a hot dog on one side and a marshmallow on the other. Definitely silly, but effective!

Materials

☆ Sticks with an approximate length of 1 yard (91 cm)
☆ Marshmallows and hot dogs
☆ Campfire ring with hot coals (page 103)
☆ Bucket filled with water

Tools

☆ Pruning shears (optional)
☆ Pocketknife

Safety Tips

☆ Always practice pocketknife safety (page 99) and campfire safety (pages 103-104).
☆ Adult supervision is recommended.
☆ Never play with fire.

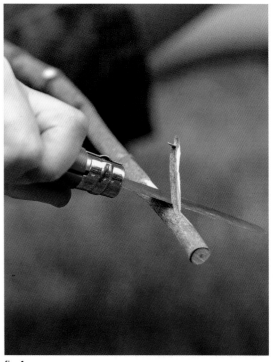

fig. 1

fig. 2

STEP 1: Search the forest floor for the perfect roasting stick. For safety reasons, try to choose a stick that is 1 yard (91 cm) in length.

If necessary, ask an adult to help you remove unnecessary branches and twigs with pruning shears.

STEP 2: Use a pocketknife to whittle the narrow end of your stick with long cuts away from your body. Continue in this fashion, rotating your stick to carve the tip into a clean point. (fig. 1 and fig. 2)

STEP 3: Soak your roasting stick in water for at least 30 minutes before using it. This will help prevent the stick from burning while you cook your food.

STEP 4: Your roasting stick is complete! Carefully slide your marshmallow or hot dog onto the stick and then roast it to golden perfection.

YOUR DESIGN CHALLENGE:

Use your pocketknife to carve a roasting stick for outdoor cooking.

Take It Further

» Roasting food over a campfire is fun! Can you think of other foods that you can cook on a stick? Grilled cheese sandwiches? Bacon? Fruit? Cheese curds? Kebabs? Oh, my stomach is rumbling just thinking about it!

» Try making a spider dog, a whacky version of cooked hot dogs that are especially fun to roast over campfires. To prepare a spider dog, simply slice a long X into each end of a hot dog. Slide the hot dog onto your roasting stick, and then cook it over hot coals. As your hot dog cooks, the ends will curl up and make your hot dog look just like an 8-legged spider! Do allow your spider dog to cool for a moment before eating it leg by leg.

Campfire Chemistry

Science is everywhere, friends . . . everywhere! Sitting around a campfire is a great place to observe and discuss physical and chemical changes.

A physical change is a type of change in which a new substance is not formed. For example, when you carve your roasting stick, you are only changing its appearance, not turning it into a new substance. No matter how much you whittle your stick, its composition will remain the same.

A burnt roasting stick, a toasted marshmallow, and the campfire itself are examples of chemical changes. When a chemical change occurs, an entirely new substance is formed. Chemical changes cannot be reversed, so no matter how hard you try, you simply can't unroast a marshmallow!

DIY Tic-Tac-Toe

▶▶➤ Sometimes after you've been playing outside for a long time,
it's nice to relax under the trees or in a fort with a book or quiet game.
Using cording, twigs, and stones, you can make a simple, nature-inspired
tic-tac-toe game. **My kids like to call it "twig"-tac-toe!**

Tic-tac-toe is a popular game, but perhaps it's new to you.
Played on a 3 x 3 grid, each player chooses whether he or she wants to be
represented by "X's" or "O's." Taking turns, each player places their "X" or "O"
on the game board in an attempt to be the first player to get three in a
row horizontally, vertically, or diagonally.

Materials

★ **4 small stones**
★ **8 twigs**
★ **4 sticks of equal size**
★ **Cording, such as twine or parachute cord**

Tools

★ **Pruning shears (optional)**
★ **Scissors or pocketknife**

Safety Tips

★ **Only adults should use the pruning shears.**

fig. 1

fig. 2

fig. 3

STEP 1: Search the forest floor for stones, twigs, and four sticks of equal size. You may need to break the sticks and twigs, or ask an adult to cut them to equal length with a pair of pruning shears. (fig. 1)

YOUR DESIGN CHALLENGE:

Create a rustic, homemade version of tic-tac-toe with sticks and stones.

STEP 2: Use the twine to tie the four sticks together into the shape of a tic-tac-toe board. (fig. 2)

STEP 3: Next, use the twine to tie two twigs together into the shape of a letter X. Repeat three more times to make a total of four game pieces shaped like the letter X. (fig. 3)

STEP 4: Your tic-tac-toe game is complete! Enjoy relaxing and playing with friends and family.

Take It Further

» Volunteer to make several tic-tac-toe games for your school playground or local community center so other kids can enjoy it too!
» Can you make any other classic games with sticks and stones? Brainstorm, sketch, and then prototype your designs!

Stick Catapult

▶▶➤ A catapult is a device that is used to propel objects. Believe it or not, **catapults are a type of simple machine called a lever.** Levers reduce the amount of force needed to lift and move objects. As you pivot the lever arm of your stick catapult around the fulcrum and stretch the rubber band, you are storing energy in the rubber band. Pulling the lever arm converts the kinetic energy of your moving arm into potential energy, or stored energy, in the rubber band.

When you let go of the lever arm, the potential energy stored inside of the rubber band is released and rapidly converted back to kinetic energy, or energy in motion. This kinetic energy then transfers to the load causing it to launch through the air.

Building a catapult from sticks is easy and fun . . . especially around the campfire (page 105). When your friend asks, "Please pass the marshmallows," you can launch one right over to him or her with your handy stick catapult!

Materials

- ☆ **8 "frame" sticks with a diameter of ½ inch (1 cm) and a length of 7 inches (18 cm)**
- ☆ **2 "base" sticks with a diameter of 1 inch (2.5 cm) and a length of 7 inches (18 cm)**
- ☆ **Superglue**
- ☆ **Plastic jar lid**
- ☆ **Cording, such as twine or parachute cord**
- ☆ **10 rubber bands**
- ☆ **Four #16 x 1" wire nails**

Tools

- ☆ **Pruning shears (optional)**
- ☆ **Scissors or a pocketknife**
- ☆ **Hammer**

→ Process

fig. 1

fig. 2

fig. 3

STEP 1: Search the forest floor for ten sticks. Ask an adult to remove excess branches or twigs from the sticks, and then trim them to the suggested length with a pair of pruning shears.

STEP 2: Ask your grown-up to help you squeeze a pea-size blob of superglue on the top of the plastic jar lid. **(fig. 1)**

STEP 3: Place the end of one "frame stick" into the glue, then set it aside to dry. This stick will serve as the lever arm, or bar, of your catapult.

STEP 4: Place two thick "base" sticks parallel to each other with about 3 inches (7.5 cm) of space in between them.

STEP 5: To build the base of the catapult, position one "frame" stick on each side of the thicker "base" sticks as if you were building a log cabin. Attach the "frame" sticks to the "base" sticks by hammering a nail into each end. **(fig. 2)**

STEP 6: Use rubber bands to help you stabilize the rest of the structure as you build. First, create a triangular shape on each side of the base,

forming the frame of the catapult. Next, secure a stick to the middle of the frame to act as the fulcrum. Then wrap cording, such as twine, around each rubber band to make the catapult appear more rustic. **(fig. 3)**

STEP 7: Position the lever arm of the catapult behind the fulcrum. Be sure the end of the lever arm is positioned in front of the base stick. Secure the lever arm to the fulcrum with a rubber band. Loosely wrap twine around the rubber band to make the catapult appear more rustic. **(fig. 4)**

fig. 4

STEP 8: Last, connect the bottom end of the lever arm to the base with a rubber band.

STEP 9: Your stick catapult is complete! Enjoy perfecting your aim as you launch soft loads, such as marshmallows and pom poms, through the air.

Garden Markers

▶▶→ Do you love to garden? My kids and I do, but sometimes
we forget the names of the plants we buy.

To solve this problem, we began carving our own little **rustic garden
markers** from backyard sticks. They are perfect for potted plants and gardens,
and make a thoughtful homemade gift for friends, teachers, and family.

Materials

☆ **Sticks that measure 9 inches (23 cm) long
and ½ inch (1 cm) across**
☆ **Wood-burning tool or waterproof paint pens**

Tools

☆ **Pruning shears (optional)**
☆ **Pocketknife**

Safety Tips

☆ **Adult supervision is
recommended.**
☆ **Only adults should use
the pruning shears.**
☆ **Work gloves can help
protect small hands.**

fig. 1

fig. 2

fig. 3

STEP 1: Gather a variety of sticks from your yard or local park. You may need to break the sticks or ask an adult to cut them to a length of about 9 inches (23 cm) with a pair of pruning shears.

STEP 2: Use your pocketknife to slice several inches off one end of the stick, leaving a flat, clean surface behind. (fig. 1)

STEP 3: Repeat step 2 until all of the sticks are prepared.

STEP 4: Use a wood-burning tool or a waterproof paint pen to write the names of your plants on the flat surface of the garden marker. (fig. 2)

TIP: If you plan to use a wood-burning tool, be sure to review the directions that came with your tool. While using the tool, it's best to write with soft, steady strokes.

STEP 5: Your stick garden markers are complete! Push the garden markers into the soil near the plants you wish to label. (fig. 3)

DID YOU KNOW?
The art of wood burning is called pyrography, which literally means writing with fire. It is believed that pyrography dates back to ancient times when early man drew symbols and designs with charred wood.

YOUR DESIGN CHALLENGE:

Use your pocketknife to carve stick garden markers.

fig. 3

Take It Further

» Pair garden markers with seed packets for a unique DIY gift.
» Experiment with using sticks from various trees. Which stick will last the longest?
» Use stick garden markers to label plants in your rock garden (page 118).

Pocketknife Safety

The most important thing you need to remember about using a pocketknife is that a pocketknife is a tool, not a toy.

Let's repeat that:

"A pocketknife is a tool, not a toy!"

Before opening your pocketknife, observe your surroundings. Are you far enough away from other people, animals, and objects to use your knife safely?

While using your pocketknife, always cut by pushing the knife away from your body. Don't forget to close your pocketknife and put it away when you are finished using it. Avoid walking with an open pocketknife or leaving your knife unattended.

Easy ROCK Projects

Rocks are all around us, and have been for billions of years! Rocks give geologists (scientists who study the Earth) clues as to what our planet was like in the past.

In this section, you'll engineer a stone bridge (page 139), practice mindfulness while creating land art (page 131), and crush sedimentary rocks to make an ancient earth paint called ochre (page 134).

So pull on your creeking shoes, grab a bucket, and then get outside to collect, create, and learn about rocks.

Build a Campfire Ring

»»→ A campfire ring can be a beautiful, rustic addition to your backyard or natural play area. My kids love sitting around campfires to roast marshmallows, share stories, and watch for shooting stars.

If you are building a campfire ring for imaginary play, it does not matter what materials you use . . . just have fun building, creating, and playing!

But if you wish to build a functional campfire ring, there are several safety and environmental considerations to be mindful of:

1. If you have the option, always use existing campfire rings rather than choosing to build a new one. (continued)

fig. 1

Materials

★ **Dry hard rocks**
★ **Bucket filled with water**

Tools

★ **Shovel**

Safety Tips

★ **Adult supervision is recommended.**
★ **Never play with fire.**
★ **Carefully review safety rules 1–5 before building your campfire.**

2. Do not light campfires during dry or windy weather, near structures, or without the presence of an adult. Keep campfires small and controlled.

3. Collect firewood from the forest floor. Firewood should be no thicker than your arm.

4. When lighting a fire within a campfire ring, it's very important to make sure the rocks of your campfire ring are dry. If the rocks are wet or contain water inside of them (like river rocks or sedimentary rocks), the water will boil and turn into steam. As the steam expands, it will put pressure on the rock and may cause it to explode. It's best to use hard rock, such as granite or marble, when building a campfire ring. Avoid using river rock or sandstone.

5. Keep a water-filled bucket nearby. Never leave a campfire unattended, and completely extinguish the fire when you are finished with it.

fig. 2

fig. 3

STEP 1: Choose a safe location for your campfire ring that is at least 10 feet (3 m) away from any structures.

STEP 2: Use a shovel to remove the grass where you plan to build your campfire ring. (fig. 1)

STEP 3: Position dry rocks in a circle around the space you cleared. We used large, hard rocks from a dry creek bed. (fig. 2)

STEP 4: To prevent burning embers from igniting natural materials outside of your campfire ring, clear the area of flammable material such as dry leaves, twigs, and other debris before lighting a fire. (fig. 3)

STEP 5: Your campfire ring is complete! Enjoy relaxing around your campfire with friends and family.

YOUR DESIGN CHALLENGE:

Build a functional and safe campfire ring.

How to Build a Campfire

There are several ways to build a campfire, but the log cabin method is our favorite. To start a campfire using the log cabin method, you first need to collect your firewood:

Tinder: Tinder is the dry material you light to create the fire. Twigs, leaves, dry grass, and pine needles are excellent natural sources of tinder. Our favorite place to collect tinder is from under pine trees.

Kindling: Kindling is the term for dry sticks that are typically the diameter of a pencil.

Fuel: Fuel is the term for firewood that is about the diameter of your arm.

BUILD YOUR CAMPFIRE

To build a log cabin fire, stack kindling into the shape of a small log cabin. Fill the inside of the log cabin with tinder, then place a "roof" of kindling and smaller fuel logs over the cabin.

Ask an adult to light the tinder. As the fire spreads from the tinder to the kindling, your adult may continue to add fuel logs to the fire.

Construct a Dam

▶▶→ As you probably know, **a dam is a type of barrier** that restricts and controls the flow of water. The main purposes of today's dams are to create electricity, prevent flooding, and to provide water for cities and farms.

Building dams in creeks is a classic activity that is loved by kids of all ages. My kids like to build creek dams to create shallow pools for minnows! Just be sure to dismantle, or take apart, your dam when you are finished playing so it does not harm wildlife or disrupt the environment.

Materials

★ **Old clothes and shoes that can get wet**
★ **Stones, in a variety of sizes**

Safety Tips

★ **Adult supervision is recommended during water activities.**

fig. 1

fig. 2

fig. 3

STEP 1: Thoughtfully select the location of your dam. We chose a narrow part of the creek where rocks and stones were plentiful.

STEP 2: Team up with friends and family to haul large rocks to your desired location, and then line them up straight across the creek. **(fig.1)**

STEP 3: Fill in the large gaps of the dam foundation with medium-size rocks. **(fig. 2)**

STEP 4: After the large gaps are filled with medium-size rocks, scoop up small pebbles and gravel from the creek bed to fill in smaller gaps. **(fig.3)**

STEP 5: Your dam is complete! Enjoy splashing in deeper water as the creek fills up and forms a pool behind your dam. **(fig. 4)**

LEAVE NO TRACE: Always dismantle dams when you are finished playing to avoid disrupting the environment.

YOUR DESIGN CHALLENGE:

Build a dam outside in a creek or shallow stream to stop or change the flow of water.

Take It Further

» Just for fun, try building a dam with logs, sticks, and mud like a beaver.
» What happens when you break your dam? Time how long it takes for your pool to empty.

fig. 4

Leaf-Stamped Stones

▶▶→ Rock hunting groups have rapidly gained popularity in cities around the world. Joining one via social media is a free and fun way to spend time with friends and family while enjoying the great outdoors.

Stamping rocks with leaves is a creative and simple way to join the rock painting movement. Bonus? Leaf-stamped rocks boast a little bit of camouflage, making them extra fun to hide and find!

Materials

* ★ **Leaves**
* ★ **Stones**
* ★ **Self-sealing acrylic paint (also known as outdoor acrylic paint)**
* ★ **Sponge paintbrushes**

fig. 1

fig. 2

fig. 3

STEP 1: Get outside with friends and family to collect leaves and stones.

STEP 2: Lightly coat the back of your leaf (the vein side) with a thin layer of acrylic paint. (fig. 1)

STEP 3: Place the leaf paint side down on top of a rock. Softly press the leaf to transfer the paint to the rock. (fig. 2)

STEP 4: Carefully peel the leaf away from the rock and then set the rock aside to dry. (fig. 3)

STEP 5: Your leaf-stamped stone is complete! Repeat steps 2–4 to create more beautiful stamped rocks.

YOUR DESIGN CHALLENGE:

After identifying and gathering native leaves, make colorful leaf-stamped stones with acrylic paint.

Take It Further

» There are so many fun ways to design with rocks! Try adding some of your leaf-stamped rocks to your land art (page 131) and see what beautiful designs you can create.

» Use a paint marker or black permanent marker to write the name of the plant the leaf stamp was created from. When people find your leaf-stamped stone, they may learn something new!

» Use your leaf-stamped stones to build backyard cairns (page 115).

Carving Stamps

Stamping is an art form that dates back to ancient times. Early stamps were carved from wood, stone, or bone.

With your grown-up's permission, use a pocketknife to carve a leaf design into a soft block of wood. Lightly coat the block of wood with paint, then press it onto a sheet of paper to make a print.

What else can you use from nature to create stamps?

How to Stack Stone Cairns

▶▶→ All across the world, humans have been **building stone cairns** since ancient times. By definition, cairns are stacks of balanced rocks traditionally used to mark graves, trails, and important landmarks.

Building a stone cairn is an engaging challenge that can help kids develop social-emotional skills such as mindfulness, patience, and persistence in a natural setting. It's also a fantastic activity for discussing science and engineering principles such as geology, gravity, balance, and creative thinking.

Materials

☆ **Stones, in a variety of shapes and sizes**

Safety Tips

☆ **Watch your toes! Consider wearing closed-toed shoes while building stone cairns because what goes up . . . must come down!**

YOUR DESIGN CHALLENGE:

After collecting stones, build a towering, balancing stone cairn.

STEP 1: Gather a variety of rocks that you wish to stack.

STEP 2: Stack the rocks from largest to smallest, paying special attention to the natural shape of the rocks and how they balance, or carry their weight.

STEP 3: Continue to add rocks to your cairn, challenging yourself to build it as high as you safely can. (fig. 1)

STEP 4: Your stone cairn is complete! Snap a picture, then carefully dismantle it and return the stones to the environment because rocks are a key habitat feature for many plants and animals.

LEAVE NO TRACE: Be a good steward—always dismantle your stone cairns when you are finished with them and carefully return the rocks to the environment from which you retrieved them. Many small creatures, such as crayfish, insects, and fish, depend upon rocks to enjoy a long and healthy life cycle.

Take It Further

» Turn your cairn into a work of art by challenging yourself to build an arch that appears to defy gravity!
» Try stacking the rocks from smallest to largest. Are you able to build your cairn as high?
» Lay a long, flat rock atop a round (or pointed) rock to make a structure that resembles a balance. Build a miniature cairn on each side of the flat rock, doing your best to keep the structure balanced and level.

fig. 1

The Rock Garden

»→ Making a rock garden is a fun project to enjoy with friends and family. It feels good to get outside to collect stones, choose plants, dig, water, and enjoy the beauty of a new garden.

Build your rock garden in your yard and fill it with annuals (plants that grow once), perennials (plants that grow back every year), or vegetables, herbs, and fruits (plants you can eat). Or, build it in your natural play area and grow native plants, ferns, and seeds you've collected on nature hikes.

Materials

★ **Large stones**
★ **Brown paper bags, such as grocery or yard waste bags**
★ **Garden soil**
★ **Plants**
★ **2 containers, such as a pail or empty flowerpot**

YOUR DESIGN CHALLENGE:

Use stones from your environment to build a rock garden.

fig. 1

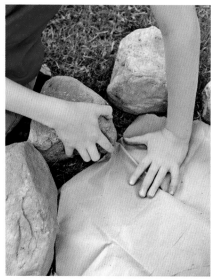

fig. 2

fig. 3

STEP 1: Carefully arrange the rocks in the area you wish to build a garden.

We created a round rock garden in the middle of our yard, but you may wish to create a garden along a fence, in your backyard, or in the corner of your yard or play area.

The amount of rocks you need will depend upon the size of your garden. Our small rock garden consisted of twelve large stones, but you may need more . . . or less. (fig. 1)

STEP 2: Lay brown paper grocery or yard waste bags on top of the grass in your garden. The combination of paper and soil will block light and help discourage weed and grass growth in your new garden. (fig. 2)

STEP 3: Use an empty flowerpot or pail to scoop the garden soil into the garden. We found it helpful to pour the garden soil into a wheelbarrow for easy access, but that is completely optional. Spread the soil around the garden with your hands.

Alternatively, you could ask an adult to help you lift the bag and pour the soil directly into the garden. (fig. 3)

STEP 4: Prepare your soil for planting by using your hands to dig a hole that is large enough to hold a plant and its entire root system.

STEP 5: Now it's time to plant! When I was a little girl, my grandmother (who was a master gardener and horticulturist) taught me to remove plants from pots by carefully placing my hand around the base of the plant, then tipping the pot so the plant and soil slides out. In some cases, you may need to gently tap or pinch the pot to help the plant break free.

fig. 4

Take It Further

» Use string to help you divide a circular rock garden into eighths, like a pizza. Enjoy planting tomatoes, oregano, basil, and garlic in each "slice" to make a pizza garden. (Too bad pepperoni can't be grown in a garden!)

» Choose plants that attract beneficial pollinators. Some ideas include butterfly weed, bee balm, coneflowers, and yarrow. Don't forget to add your DIY Bug Hotel (page 28) to the garden!

STEP 6: Use the tips of your fingers to gently loosen the plant's bound roots. Loosening the roots will help the plant grow and thrive in its new environment.

STEP 7: Place the plant in the hole, fill in the hole with soil, and then gently pat the freshly planted area. Repeat steps 4–7 until your entire garden is planted! (fig. 4)

STEP 8: Water your garden with a hose or watering can.

HOW TO CARE FOR NEW PLANTS:
When your garden is new, you should take care to water the plants daily for 1 to 2 weeks. As the plants grow and establish deeper roots, water every other day or 2 to 3 times/week, depending on the weather and your plant's needs.

STEP 9: Your rock garden is complete! Enjoy caring for your plants and watching them change throughout the season.

Make and Use Stone Tools

▶▶→ Millions of years ago, early humans made one of the most important advancements in human history: they began to use tools.

A tool is an object designed to serve a specific function. For example, a handsaw is designed to cut wood. A hammer is designed to pound and pull nails. Can you name other tools and their functions?

Early tools were created from stone, bone, or shell. In this activity, you will learn how to make a basic pounding tool from a stick, stone, and cording.

Materials

☆ **Medium-size stones**
☆ **Sticks with a 1-inch (2.5-cm) diameter**
☆ **Cording, such as twine or parachute cord**
☆ **1 log pillar with a diameter of 4–5 inches (10–13 cm)**
☆ **17 x ¾" wire nails**
☆ **Pencil**
☆ **Red embroidery floss**
☆ **Heart-shaped cookie cutter**

Tools

☆ **Scissors or pocketknife**
☆ **Pruning shears (optional)**

Safety Tips

☆ **Work gloves can help protect small hands.**
☆ **Wear eye protection while using tools.**

fig. 1

Take It Further

» Experiment with using stones of varying texture and size. Is one type of stone better suited for a specific task?
» Visit a history museum to see authentic stone natural tools and other artifacts from early humans.

YOUR DESIGN CHALLENGE:

Use sticks and stones to make stone tools, and then use them to pound nails.

STEP 1: Gather several medium-size stones and a handful of sticks with a 1-inch (2.5-cm) diameter. If necessary, ask an adult to trim the sticks to equal lengths with a pair of pruning shears.

STEP 2: Lash a rock to a stick by wrapping the cording around both objects in a diagonal fashion (lash from the top left corner to the bottom right corner). Wrap the cording 3 to 5 times. (fig. 1)

STEP 3: Change directions by wrapping the cording around both objects from the top right corner to the bottom left corner 3 to 5 times. When you are finished, your lashing should be in the shape of an X.

STEP 4: Tie off the cording, and then remove any excess with a pocket-knife or scissors.

STEP 5: Your stone tool is complete! Enjoy using your stone tool to pound nails, pegs, or sticks.

String Art Heart Craft

Put your stone pounding tool to the test! Learn how to create heart string art, a colorful and fun nature craft for kids.

To make it, trace the outline of a heart-shaped cookie cutter onto a log pillar. Use your stone tool to pound 17 x ³⁄₄" wire nails along the outline. When you are finished, wrap red embroidery floss around the nails.

Crafty Stone Pendant

▶▶→ Start **saving beautiful rocks** from your nature adventures, because making stone pendants is an easy and fun way to be creative and show off your best rock finds.

Before you begin, be sure to wash your stones in warm, soapy water. My kids use an inexpensive dish scrub brush to remove dirt and plant matter from their rocks. When the rocks are clean, allow them to dry in the sun for several hours before moving on with the steps that follow.

Materials

- ☆ **Cording, such as twine**
- ☆ **Clear acrylic buttons**
- ☆ **Superglue**
- ☆ **Small smooth stones, such as river rock**
- ☆ **Painted wooden beads**

Tools

- ☆ **Scissors**
- ☆ **Protective gloves (optional, but recommended)**

Safety Tips

- ☆ **Consider wearing protective gloves and eye protection while using the superglue.**

fig. 1

fig. 2

fig. 3

STEP 1: After gathering supplies, use the scissors to cut a 2-foot (61 cm) length of twine. **(fig. 1)**

STEP 2: Thread the twine through the clear button, centering the button in the center of the twine. **(fig. 2)**

STEP 3: Ask an adult to help you squeeze a pea-size blob of super-glue on the flat side of the button.

STEP 4: Press the button glue-side-down onto the upper center of your rock, being careful not to get any super glue on your skin or clothes.

In fact, you and your grown-up may wish to wear gloves for this part! **(fig. 3)**

DID YOU KNOW?
Humans have been making and wearing pendants since the Stone Age. Long ago, pendants were often made from stones, shells, and even teeth or bone! Sometimes pendants were believed to be amulets or talismans, and were thought to give protection against evil and bring the wearer good luck. If you have a "lucky rock," you may enjoy using it to make your very own magical amulet.

YOUR DESIGN CHALLENGE:

Make a pendant with stone, string, and simple craft supplies.

STEP 5: When the glue is dry, pull the strings together and thread three wooden beads on them.

STEP 6: Your stone pendant is complete! Pull the twine apart and ask an adult to help you tie it around your neck. Cut off any excess twine and enjoy.

fig. 4

Take It Further

» Decorate your stones with acrylic paint or paint markers.
» Make a pendant with a Leaf-Stamped Stone, as seen on page 110.
» Try making more stone jewelry, such as bracelets and rings.

TIP: My kids prefer to keep their stone pendants loose so they can pull them on and off all by themselves. If you would like to do the same, simply knot the twine in a place where you can still pull the stone pendant over your head. (fig. 4)

Make Land Art

▶▶→ In this activity, we are going to relax, breathe deeply,
and embrace an attitude of gratitude by **creating land art** with sticks,
stones, and other natural objects.

Land art, or earth art, is art that is created directly on land with
natural elements. It can be as simple as drawing a design in wet sand with a piece
of driftwood, or as complex as building massive sculptures with stone or wood.
Some historians suggest that Stonehenge, a monument in England,
is a form of prehistoric earth art.

Materials

☆ **Sticks, in a variety of sizes and colors**
☆ **Stones, in a variety of sizes and colors**
☆ **Additional natural objects, such as pine cones,
pine needles, leaves, flowers, seedpods, berries,
nuts, moss, and feathers**
☆ **An empty container to collect natural materials, such as a basket, pail, or shoebox**

fig. 1

fig. 2

STEP 1: First you will need to decide upon a location for your land art. Perhaps you've found a lovely spot in the dirt under a tree, or maybe on top of an old tree stump? Sidewalks are also convenient places to build land art.

Wherever you choose, it helps to use your hands to clear the area of natural debris. Think of it as wiping off a chalkboard or getting a fresh sheet of drawing paper.

STEP 2: After you've chosen the location for your land art, scour the ground for natural objects such as sticks, stones, pine cones, pine needles, leaves, flowers, seedpods, berries, nuts, moss, and feathers.

Place your nature finds into an empty container, then head back to where you plan to create your art.

STEP 3: Begin building your land art! It's always helpful to build your land art from the center out. Choose a beautiful stone to be the center of your land art, or perhaps a flower or acorn.

As you place the centerpiece of your land art, breathe deeply and think of something or someone you feel grateful for.

DID YOU KNOW?
Circular land art with a design that radiates from the center is often called a mandala. By definition, a mandala is a Hindu or Buddhist symbol of the universe. Throughout history, people have used mandalas to aid meditation and spiritual journeys, or to focus attention. On your next nature walk, look for natural mandalas. You may find them on (or inside) plants, flowers, spiderwebs, shells, fruits, and seeds. Let natural mandalas inspire your land art!

Take It Further

» Invite a friend to build large-scale land art with you.
» Challenge yourself to build upward, as well as outward.
» Make a photo book of your land art designs.
» Build land art in a spiral design.

STEP 4: With each deep breath, continue adding natural objects to your land art, working symmetrically from the center out. As you place each item, continue naming people and things you feel thankful for.

STEP 5: Your land art is complete! Snap a picture, then return your natural objects to the environment.

TIP: If your land art is 100% natural and not disruptive or impeding a path, you may wish to leave it out for others to discover and enjoy. Many land artists leave their earth art and allow it to blow away, decompose, or become covered with new plant growth over time.

Mindful Techniques

If you feel stressed, sad, or angry, your brain's natural fight, flight, or freeze response kicks in, making rational decision-making nearly impossible.

Creating land art is a useful mindfulness tool that can give you space and time to calm down and pay attention to what is going on in your body and the environment.

Regularly practicing mindfulness techniques while choosing an attitude of gratitude can reduce stress and increase wellness and self-control.

Earthy Ochre Paint

➤➤ Ochre is an earth pigment containing iron oxide, typically found in clays and sedimentary rocks such as shale or sandstone. Traditionally used in cave paintings, as body paint, and even as makeup, ochre can be yellow, red, or deep brown in color.

In this activity, you will learn how to make ochre paint with sedimentary rock; rock that is formed when layers of sediment—pebbles, sand, minerals, plant and animal matter—collect and compress over time.

When you are finished painting, it's best to let your paint air dry (no lid) within the container to prevent mold growth. When you wish to use your paint again, simply add water and stir with a spoon or craft stick.

Materials

- ☆ Sedimentary rocks, such as shale or sandstone, in a variety of colors
- ☆ Mortar and pestle
- ☆ Small spoon or craft stick
- ☆ 2 small glass jars or containers
- ☆ Water
- ☆ Plastic dropper
- ☆ Paintbrush
- ☆ Paper
- ☆ Liquid glycerin (optional)

YOUR DESIGN CHALLENGE:

After identifying and gathering local sedimentary rocks, prepare and paint with ochre paint.

fig. 1

fig. 2

fig. 3

STEP 1: Gather a variety of sedimentary rocks. We always have the best luck finding sedimentary rocks, such as gray, brown, and red shale near creek beds.

STEP 2: Place a small piece of rock inside of the mortar, then grind it into a fine powder with the pestle. **(fig. 1)**

STEP 3: Use a spoon to scoop the powder into a small glass jar. Fill your second glass jar with water. **(fig. 2)**

STEP 4: Use a plastic dropper to transfer water into the jar that contains the powder. Stir occasionally with a spoon or craft stick to check the consistency of the mixture, adding more water or powder as you see fit. **(fig. 3)**

The consistency of your paint should be similar to commercial paint, albeit a tad grittier! **(fig. 4)**

TIP: If you want your paints to resemble watercolors, simply add more water.

STEP 5: If desired, add a small amount of liquid glycerin to your paint mixture. The glycerin will help your paint feel smoother while extending the length of time it takes to dry.

STEP 6: Your ochre paint is complete. Simply dip your brush into the paint and enjoy making art with your colorful earth pigment!

fig. 4

Create Ochre Cave Art

Ask your grown-up to help you hop online to research the Lascaux cave paintings. These famous Paleolithic ochre cave paintings in France depict images of native animals, symbols, and human figures. They are more than 20,000 years old!

To make art reminiscent of early cave paintings, use your ochre paints on top of stone, sandpaper, or a crinkled brown paper grocery bag. Paint animals and plants that are native to your environment. In addition to using your ochre paints, try drawing with charred wood leftover from your campfire (page 105).

Take It Further

» Nature is an amazing source of natural colors! What else can you use to make natural paint? Can you make paint with edible berries, mud, or plants?
» Experiment with using your ochre paint on textured surfaces, such as wood, canvas, or stone.
» Try mixing your ochre paint with a different liquid, such as milk or oil. How does this change the consistency of the paint?
» Set aside your paintbrush and try painting with your fingers, sticks, flowers, feathers, and pine needles.

Build a Simple Stone Bridge

▶▶➔ When I was a little girl, there was a section of trail in the woods behind our home that flooded after heavy rainfall. To get across the squishy grass and mud, my brothers and I built a bridge with rocks. We used to pretend that the squelching mud was hot lava and hopping from stone to stone was the only safe way to cross to the other side of our adventure!

Building a bridge—a structure that enables safe passage over obstacles—above creeks, puddles, and muddy trails is a fun, collaborative engineering project for kids of all ages.

Not only will you develop engineering, teamwork, and problem-solving skills, but you will also learn: **1)** how bridges work **2)** how bridges help people and **3)** which natural materials you can use to build a bridge.

Materials
☆ **Rocks, in a variety of shapes and sizes**

Safety Tips
☆ **Adult supervision is recommended during water activities.**

fig. 1

Build a simple stone bridge over water or mud.

STEP 1: Choose a location for your bridge. As you think about building your bridge, consider it's length, function, and how your bridge will be used.

STEP 2: Place a large rock in the water (or mud) near dry land. (fig. 1)

STEP 3: Continue adding large rocks in a row until you reach the opposite side. Be sure your stone bridge isn't impeding the natural flow of water in any way. (fig. 2)

TIP: If you want your feet to stay dry, walk back and forth on the rocks you've already placed while building.

STEP 4: Your stone bridge is complete! Enjoy traveling on the rocks to reach your destination, all the while staying clean and dry!

DID YOU KNOW?

People have been building bridges from cut wood or stone for centuries. The Ancient Romans revolutionized bridge-building efforts when they introduced arches. Strong arch bridges invited trade, travel, and the growth of new cities.

fig. 2

Take It Further

» As you walk across your stone bridge, observe if any of the stones feel wobbly. What could you do to stabilize the rocks in your bridge?

» Try your hand at building a miniature stone arch bridge. It's harder than it looks!

» What other natural materials can you use for bridge building? Try building a simple log beam bridge by positioning a log over a creek or stream.

Acknowledgments

This book was a very big, exciting project! I feel incredibly grateful for the encouragement and support of my friends, family, and publishing team. Special thanks to:

My husband, Todd, who cheered me on, modeled for photos, and even hauled logs, branches, and rocks out of the forest for me.

All the kids—Colin, Owen, Leah, Juliet, Smith, Ryan, Rebecca, Landon, Lexi, Karina, Natalie, Hayden, Noah, Naomi, and Luke—for always being ready for an outdoor adventure!

My Crafty Tribe—Kim, Chelsey, Rachel, Agnes, Andreja, Samantha, Stef, Helen, Maggy, Kate, Bonnie, Susie, Penny, Kate, Emma, and Rodrigo—for your generosity and friendship.

My brothers, Brian and Kevin, who made sure I accurately described the stick fishing pole and catapult activities.

Thom O'Hearn, Dennis Pernu, Heather Godin, Renae Haines, and the entire team at Quarry Books for your patience, creativity, and confidence.

My parents, Bob and Donna Japp, who raised me to love the great outdoors.

About the Author

Originally from upstate New York, Melissa Lennig used to sneak out of her bed at night to sleep under the stars.

After working as an outdoor educator and elementary school counselor for nearly ten years, she left her job to follow her love of writing, photography, and creating. Eager to share her passion for outdoor play, crafting, and social-emotional learning with others, she founded the popular blog *Fireflies and Mud Pies*.

Melissa loves creeking, science museums, photographing insects, gardening, and creating fun projects for her boys. She currently lives in Columbus, Ohio with her family and yellow lab.

She graduated from St. John Fisher College where she studied elementary education and English. Melissa received her master's degree in counselor education from Marywood University.

To see more of Melissa's outdoor play ideas and easy craft projects, visit FirefliesandMudPies.com.

Index